DISCOVER THE
DIFFERENCE

Lion and Tiger

RIGBY
INTERACTIVE
LIBRARY

This edition © 1997 Rigby Education
Published by Rigby Interactive Library,
an imprint of Rigby Education,
division of Reed Elsevier, Inc.
500 Coventry Lane
Crystal Lake, IL 60014

Printed in Britain

Library of Congress Cataloging-in-Publication Data
Theodorou, Rod.
    Lion and tiger / Rod Theodorou and Carole Telford.
        p. cm. — (Discover the difference)
    Includes index.
    Summary: Compares and contrasts the physical attributes, habits,
and habitat of lions and tigers.
    ISBN 1-57572-103-1
    1. Lions—Juvenile literature. 2. Tigers—Juvenile literature. [1. Lions.
2. Tigers.] I. Telford, Carole, 1961– . II. Title. III. Series: Theodorou, Rod.
Discover the difference.
QL737.C23T4735 1996
599.74'428—dc20   96-7235

Designed by Susan Clarke
Illustrations by Adam Abel

Acknowledgments
The publisher would like to thank the following for permission to reproduce photographs: Mandal Ranjit/FLPA,
p. 7; T. Whittaker/FLPA, p. 8; Arthus Bertrand/Ardea London Ltd., p. 9; Frank Sneidermeyer/OSF, p. 4;
Bob Bennet/OSF, p. 5; Purdy & Matthews/Survival Anglia, pp. 6, 10, Planet Earth Pictures, p. 22; Gerard
Lacz/NHPA, pp. 11, 21; Jonathan Scott/Planet Earth Pictures, p. 12 *top*; Stephen Krasemann/NHPA,
p. 12 *bottom*; Anup Shah/ Planet Earth Pictures, p. 13; Ferrero, Labat/Ardea London Ltd., pp. 3, 17, 20
top, 23; P. Perry/FLPA, p. 14; E. & D. Hosking/FLPA, p. 15 *bottom*; Charles McDougal/Ardea London Ltd.,
p. 15 *top*; Roger Tidman/NHPA, p. 16; Clem Haagner/Ardea Photographics, p. 18; Ralph & Daphne
Keller/NHPA, p. 19 *top*; Ardea London Ltd., p. 19 *bottom*; W. Wisniewski/FLPA, p. 20 *bottom*.

Cover photograph reproduced with permission of Planet Earth Pictures, *top*;
Mandal Ranjit/FLPA, *bottom*.

Note to the Reader
Some words in this book are printed in **bold** type. This indicates that the word is
listed in the glossary on page 24. The glossary gives a brief explanation of words
that may be new to you and tells you the page on which each word first appears.

Contents

Introduction

The cats we keep as pets are close **relations** of the big wild cats. All cats behave in very similar ways. They are almost all carnivores—they only eat meat. They are all fast, expert hunters. Cats have short, powerful jaws and long teeth for tearing meat. They also have sharp claws to get a good grip on their **prey,** the animals they hunt.

A male lion

It's amazing!

Although the lion is often called "king of the beasts," it usually will run away from angry rhinos or elephants.

Lions and tigers are the biggest members of the cat family. The male lion has a huge mane of hair around its neck. This mane protects its neck in fights and makes it look even bigger and stronger. Tigers are the biggest and strongest of all the cats. While lions work together as a team to hunt their prey, tigers hunt alone.

The Siberian tiger is the largest of the five different kinds of tigers.

Habitat

Lions live in the dry grasslands of Africa. The weather there has only two **seasons**: wet and dry. In the wet season there are lots of large animals for lions to hunt. In the dry season many of these animals **migrate**, moving up to hundreds of miles in search of water. Lions have to hunt smaller animals and may even starve during the dry season.

Although their cubs may be killed by other animals, such as hyenas, adult lions have no real enemies in the wild—except people. The hunting of lions has stopped in many areas, but people are taking over the grasslands to farm them, pushing lions out of their territories.

This map shows where lions and tigers live today. Some lions survive in a reserve in northwest India.

A lioness watches a herd of zebra.

Where tigers live
Where lions live

Tigers live in the hot jungles of Asia, the dry forests and grasslands of India, and the cold, rocky mountains of Siberia. Each kind of tiger has a slightly different coat. The Siberian tiger needs a thicker coat than the others to keep it warm.

Tigers, like lions, have been hunted and pushed out of their **habitats,** or living areas, by people. Tigers are now an **endangered species.** Soon, some types of tigers may be gone forever.

It's amazing!

Although the Bengal tiger is the most common of all tigers, there are only about 3,000 of them left in the whole world.

This Bengal tiger is in its grasslands habitat.

Teeth, Claws, and Paws

Lions and tigers have thirty teeth, designed to help them catch, kill, and eat their prey. They have four long canine teeth to stab and hold their prey. They have incisor teeth at the front that are small but sharp enough to break through the tough skin of a buffalo or a zebra. Their back molar teeth are as sharp as scissors to slice through meat. The whole jaw is short and powerful. Lions and tigers can bite through bones!

A tiger's teeth

canine

molar

incisor

Lions and tigers have deadly curved claws. Most of the time these are pulled back (retracted) into the paw. This keeps them safe and sharp. Retracted claws make no noise as big cats sneak up on their prey. When it is time to attack, the cats can flick out their claws to grip and slash. Lions and tigers also use their claws to climb trees.

How retractable claws work

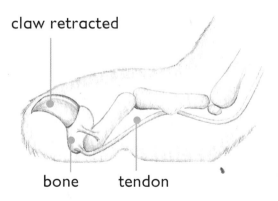

claw retracted

bone   tendon

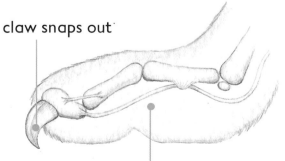

claw snaps out

tendon pulled back by leg muscle

Hunting

Lionesses are faster than male lions, so they do most of the hunting. These lionesses are chasing a gazelle.

Lions hunt gazelles, zebras, and wildebeests. All these animals can run fast. Their speed, and the fact that the grasslands of Africa are open and have hiding places, make them hard to catch. Lions work together as a team. They surround their prey on different sides and then creep up on them. They choose the youngest and weakest animals in a group.

It's amazing!
Lions are the only cats that hunt together as a team.

Tigers also are fast and expert hunters. They hunt deer, pigs, buffalo, and even baby elephants. If they are very hungry, they also will eat monkeys, frogs, and ants. Tigers hunt alone at night. Their eyesight is six times better than ours. They often wait by **waterholes** to **ambush** an animal that stops to drink.

Tigers are strong swimmers. They catch and eat fish and water birds, as well as land animals.

Attacking Prey

When lions attack, they try to trip or knock down their prey. They need to kill large and dangerous animals like buffalo quickly, without fighting. They usually bite the throat, which breaks the neck or quickly **suffocates** the animal. The males feed first. Then the females and the cubs feed.

A lioness grabs a wildebeest by the throat.

A family of lions kills one or two animals a week.

Tigers also leap on their prey and go for the throat. They drag their prey to a safe, hidden place to eat. Often the dead animal is too big for the tiger to eat all at once. Tigers sometimes cover the body with earth and grass and come back to feed on it the next night.

Tigers often kill several animals in a week.

Staying Hidden

Lions need to stay hidden when they creep up on their prey. A lioness' sandy yellow coat is good **camouflage** to keep her hidden against the dry grass, sun, and shade. Male lions cannot hide as easily—their dark mane is easier to spot.

It's amazing!
Lion cubs have spots that make them hard to see in the low grass and bushes.

A lioness hides in the long grass.

Tigers seem too brightly colored to hide, but in the jungles of India and Asia they are wonderfully camouflaged. A tiger's reddish-brown coat blends in with the leafy forests and grasslands, where the stripes look like the shadows of leaves and branches.

Bengal tigers are hard to see in the open and are even harder to see in the long grass!

Family Life

A family of lions is called a *pride*. Each pride has a **territory** of land on which it hunts. A pride usually is made up of about three or four males, ten or more females, and cubs. The strongest males defend the pride against attacks from hyenas and other male lions intruding on the territory. The lionesses do all the hunting. Most of the day male lions do nothing but lie in the shade and keep cool.

It's amazing!
Lions spend up to twenty hours a day resting!

A pride of lions

*Two tigers share
a wild pig.*

Tigers usually live alone, although
some male and female tigers may
live together for a while. Each tiger
has a large hunting territory. A
male tiger will sometimes share his
territory with one or two females
and even share his kill with them.

Defending Territory

The strongest male lions lead the pride. Male cubs stay with the pride until they are about three years old, when the leaders drive them away. They live alone for two or three years, until they are big enough to try to join a pride by driving out one of the leaders. The males roar at each other until the weaker lion is driven away. Sometimes they fight.

Sometimes male lions who have left the pride hunt together. Few survive because they don't hunt as well as lionesses.

It's amazing!

If a new lion takes over a pride, he will sometimes kill the old leader's cubs.

Male tigers defend their territory from other males. They will sometimes snarl and roar at other males to drive them away. When a tiger snarls, it turns its ears down to show the white patches on the back of the ears. This is a warning sign! Sometimes tigers also will fight.

Two Bengal tigers fight in the water.

This Bengal tiger snarls and turns its ears down as a warning.

Cubs

When a female lion is about to have her cubs, she leaves the pride and finds a safe place. She usually has two or three cubs. They are tiny and do not open their eyes for the first two weeks. Their mother guards them from other big cats and hyenas. After six weeks they all go back to live with the pride, and the other lionesses help to feed and guard the cubs.

Cubs learn how to hunt and kill by playing and fighting.

It's amazing!

If a lioness dies, the other females in the pride look after her cubs.

A lioness watches over her cubs.

Tigers also have two or three cubs. The mother stays away from other tigers and hides her cubs when she goes out hunting. Male tigers sometimes will kill cubs, even their own. The cubs stay with their mother for about two years, learning how to hunt and kill by watching her.

A tigress carrying her cub by the scruff (loose fold of skin) at the back of the neck.

Fact File

Lion

Weight
A male lion may weigh up to 690 pounds.

Habitat
Lions live in Africa and northwest India.

Food
Lions eat zebras, antelope, gazelles, wildebeests, giraffes, buffalo, and sometimes smaller animals.

Life Span
Lions live from 15 to 20 years.

Tiger

Weight
A male Siberian, the largest tiger, can weigh up to 846 pounds.

Habitat
Tigers live in India, Asia, Siberia.

Food
Tigers eat deer, pigs, buffalo, baby elephants, birds, fish, and other, smaller animals, even insects.

Life Span
Tigers live from 15 to 20 years.

Records
One male Siberian held in captivity grew to almost 11 feet long and weighed 932 pounds!

Glossary

ambush a surprise attack   11

camouflage colored or shaped in a way that makes an animal hard to see   14

endangered species a group of living things whose numbers are so few that they may all die out and become extinct   7

habitat the place in which an animal lives   7

migrate to move from one area to another   6

prey an animal that is hunted by another for food   4

relations a very similar group of animals   4

seasons parts of the year that have different weather (like summer and winter)   6

suffocate to stop another animal from breathing   12

territory an area that an animal defends against other animals of the same species   16

waterhole a pond or part of a river where wild animals come to drink   11

Index

Further Readings

Irvine, Georgeanne. *Blanca and Arusha: Tales of Two Big Cats.* Simon & Schuster, 1995.

MacDonald, Suse. *Nanta's Lion: A Search-and-Find Adventure.* William Morrow,1995.

Mostacchi, Massimo. *The Beast and the Boy.* North-South, 1995.